# NARWHALS

## THE WHALE DISCOVERY LIBRARY

Sarah Palmer

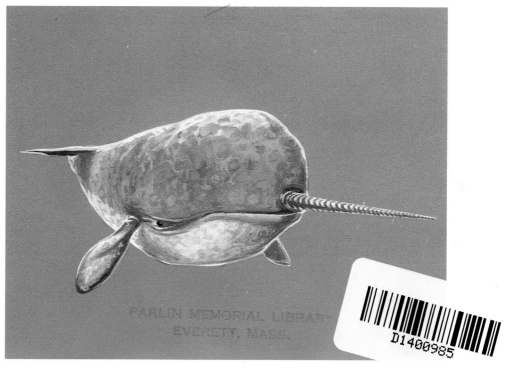

PARLIN MEMORIAL LIBRARY
EVERETT, MASS.

Illustrated by Sally Hadler

Rourke Enterprises, Inc.
Vero Beach, Florida 32964

J 599.53
Palmer

CR

© 1988 Rourke Enterprises, Inc.

All rights reserved. No part of this book
may be reproduced or utilized in any form
or by any means, electronic or mechanical
including photocopying, recording or by any
information storage and retrieval system
without permission in writing from the
publisher.

**Library of Congress Cataloging-in-Publication Data**

Palmer, Sarah, 1955-
  Narwhals.

  (The Whale discovery library)
  Includes index.
  Summary: Introduces the physical appearance,
habits, diet and habitat of this toothed whale and
threats to its existence.
  1. Narwhal—Juvenile literature.  [1. Narwhal.
  2. Whales]  I. Title.  II. Series:
Palmer, Sarah, 1955-
Whale discovery library.
QL737.C433P34  1989        599.5'3        88-3240
ISBN 0-86592-476-7

# TABLE OF CONTENTS

302880

# NARWHALS

Narwhals are very easy to recognize. Male narwhals have a long **tusk** which grows from one side of the mouth. Imagine that your top left front tooth is growing outward in front of you. That is where the narwhal's tusk grows from. Narwhals are **toothed whales**.

*Male narwhals can grow up to 18 feet long*

## HOW THEY LOOK

Narwhals are quite small whales. They rarely weigh more than a ton. Narwhals can grow up to 18 feet long. The tusk of the male narwhal is usually about 6 to 9 feet long. Female narwhals do not have a tusk. Narwhals are pale brown with darker brown spots on their backs. They do not have a **dorsal fin**.

*Female narwhals do not have tusks*

## WHERE THEY LIVE

Narwhals live in the Arctic Ocean east of Canada. They like very cold temperatures. Narwhals remain in the Arctic seas year-round. They do not **migrate** to warmer seas during the winter. As the ice melts in the summer, the narwhals move farther north into the Arctic. They like to dive right under the ice. When the narwhals need to breathe, they come up through holes in the ice.

*Narwhals live in the cold Arctic Ocean*

## WHAT THEY EAT

Narwhals are toothed whales. Toothed whales are able to grip large creatures in their teeth. Narwhals eat cod and other large fish. They also eat squid, cuttlefish, and **crustaceans** such as shrimp. The male narwhal's long tusk does not seem to get in the way when he hunts.

302880

*Narwhals eat fish and crustaceans*

*Narwhals are some of the
smallest whales*

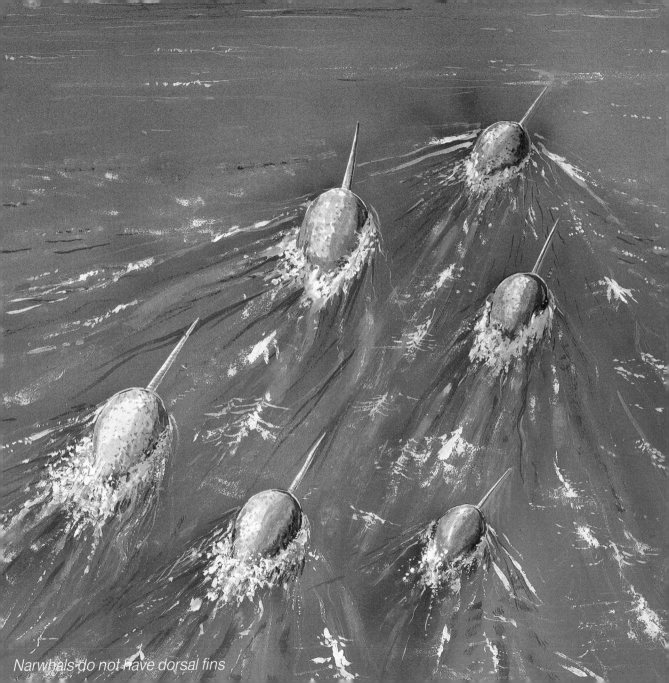

Narwhals do not have dorsal fins

## LIVING IN THE OCEAN

Narwhals share their cold home with a variety of Arctic creatures. While they feed on the many fish, the narwhals are **prey** for some of the larger animals. Sometimes the tusk of the male narwhal will give away his hiding place under the ice. He may be spotted by a polar bear. The hungry bear will attack and eat the narwhal.

*Polar bears are known to attack narwhals*

## BABY NARWHALS

The narwhals' mating season is in April. The narwhal **calves** are born in July or August the following year. They are born with only a thin layer of **blubber** or fat, one inch thick. As the young narwhals grow, their blubber becomes thicker. Narwhal calves remain close to their mothers for eighteen months.

*Narwhal calves stay very close to their mothers*

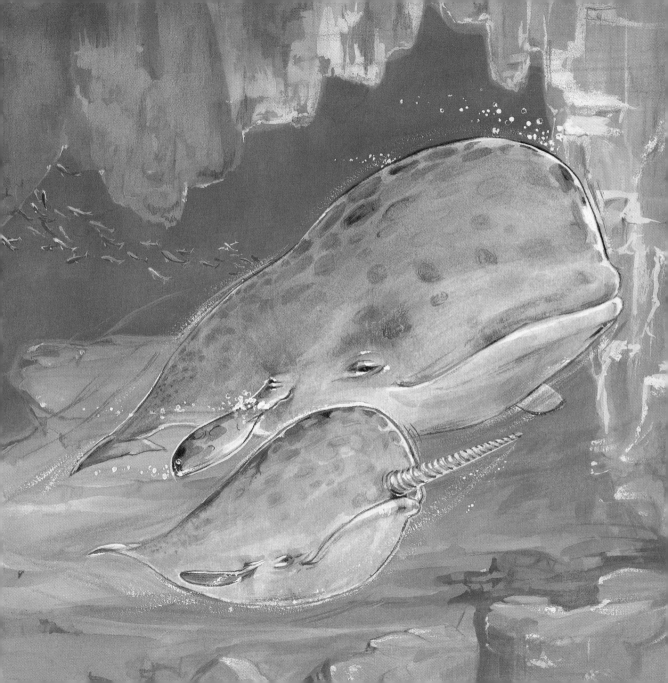

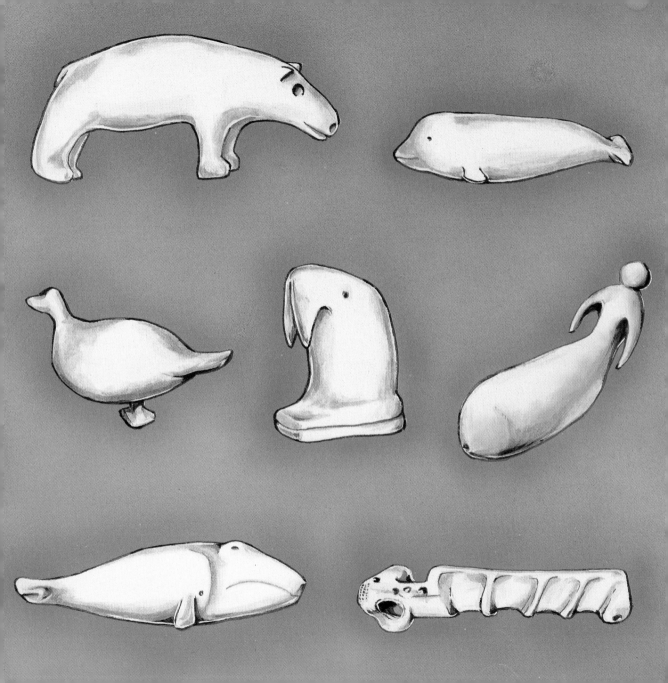

## NARWHALS AND PEOPLE

Narwhals have always been highly prized by people. Eskimos hunt narwhals for their tusks. Like elephants' tusks, narwhal tusks are made of **ivory**. With their delicately spiraled pattern, narwhal tusks can be carved into beautiful ornaments. The Chinese believe that narwhal tusks have special powers. They use them to make medicine.

*Narwhals' tusks are made of ivory*

## SAVING THE NARWHAL

There are probably about 30,000 narwhals left in the world. They are only found in the Arctic. Narwhals have been heavily hunted by the Eskimos. The Eskimos use every part of a narwhal. They eat the meat and use the blubber for oil. The skin is very rich in **vitamins** and has a delicious sweet taste. The Eskimos eat narwhal skin raw. They kill about 500 narwhals each year.

*Narwhal meat is very rich in vitamins*

# FACT FILE

Common Name:        Narwhal
Scientific Name:    Monodon monoceros
Type:               Toothed whale
Color:              Pale brown with dark
                    markings
Size:               up to 18 feet
Weight:             up to 1 ton
Number in World:    about 30,000

## Glossary

**blubber** (BLUB ber) — a thick layer of fat under a whale's skin

**calves** (CALVES) — young whales

**crustaceans** (crust A ceans) — sea animals with hard shells such as crabs and lobsters

**dorsal fin** (DOR sal FIN) — a fin on a whale's back

**ivory** (I vor y) — the hard, cream-colored tusk of an elephant, walrus or narwhal

**to migrate** (MI grate) — to move from one place to another, usually at the same time each year

**prey** (PREY) — an animal hunted by another for food

**tusk** (TUSK) — a long, pointed tooth which sticks out from the mouth

**toothed whale** (TOOTHED WHALE) — a whale which has teeth used for feeding

**vitamins** (VI ta mins) — substances needed for healthy growth

## INDEX

PARLIN MEMORIAL LIBRARY

3 1759 00050 6059